NATIONAL GEOGRAPHIC

Ladders

Mount RUSHMORE
AMERICAN WONDERS

2 Welcome to Mount Rushmore! *History Article*
by Debbie Nevins

12 The Faces on the Mountain *Social Studies Article*
by David Holford

18 Blasting Through *Social Studies Article*
by Jennifer A. Smith

24 Mount Rushmore or Six Grandfathers? *Opinion Piece*
by Debbie Nevins

30 Rushmore Rocks! *Photo Essay*
by Jennifer A. Smith

32 Discuss

Welcome to Mount Rushm

by Debbie Nevins

> Mount Rushmore is lit up at night from mid-August to May. It is located in South Dakota's Black Hills.

The Man with the Plan

Few places in the world feature giant heads carved into rock like Mount Rushmore. Set in the Black Hills of South Dakota, this American wonder showcases the heads of four "giants" of history: Presidents George Washington, Thomas Jefferson, Abraham Lincoln, and Theodore Roosevelt. Their images are carved into the hard granite of this mountain face, making Mount Rushmore one of the world's largest sculptures. Let's look back in history to see how these massive sculptures got there.

In 1923, Doane Robinson of South Dakota had a dream. He imagined a huge memorial honoring western heroes—cowboys and Native Americans together. And the memorial would be carved into a mountain.

∧ Doane Robinson

Robinson's dream was also related to his job. He was the state's official historian. As part of his job, he wanted to attract **tourists** to South Dakota. Tourists would bring money to the state. That would benefit the people and businesses of South Dakota.

Carving a colossal sculpture into a mountain was a daring goal. What made Robinson even think it was possible?

The Search Begins

To turn his dream into reality, Robinson needed an artist. Gutzon Borglum, a sculptor with experience carving mountains, was the perfect person for the job. On Stone Mountain in Georgia, Borglum had begun carving an image of heroes from the Civil War. He had also created many sculptures of other American heroes, including one of Abraham Lincoln, which was on display in the White House.

Borglum immediately loved Robinson's larger-than-life idea for South Dakota. Borglum was a man who thought big—really big. Together, the two dreamers set out into the Black Hills to find the right mountain.

∨ Harney Peak

> Gutzon Borglum was born in Idaho in 1867. After studying in Europe, he became a famous sculptor in the United States.

∧ The Needles

Monumental Mountains

Robinson and Borglum visited several locations in South Dakota to find the perfect place for the monument. Robinson's first choice was a place with jagged spikes of rock called "the Needles." They considered other South Dakota mountains—Mount Baldy, Sugarloaf, and the highest point in the state, Harney Peak. Although all of these places were impressive, Borglum didn't like any of them for his monument. Like any true artist, he was thinking about the effects of light and shadow on his work. He really wanted to find a mountain wall that faced east so the sun would shine brightly on the sculptures in the morning. They would have to keep searching.

The Perfect Spot

When Borglum saw the massive wall of rock called Mount Rushmore, he knew he had found his mountain in South Dakota. The granite surface offered the sculptor a broad space to work—about 400 feet high and 500 feet across.

This would be Borglum's masterpiece. The project and location was worthy of a larger subject than just Western heroes, Borglum told Robinson. Its topic needed to be as grand as the United States itself. He would carve the greatest American presidents: Washington, Jefferson, Lincoln, and Roosevelt. Robinson agreed— presidents were a better focus for the giant sculpture than cowboys. The men moved forward with their new plan.

In 1885, a lawyer named Charles Rushmore visited this mountain. He asked a local man its name. The man believed the mountain had no name, but suggested naming it after Rushmore. The name stuck.

Borglum studied portraits and written descriptions of the presidents to make his scale models.

First, Borglum and his team had to get permission from the South Dakota state government to carve up a mountain. They also had to somehow raise enough money from private donations to pay for the carving. That didn't go very well. Then President Calvin Coolidge promised that the U.S. government would fund the project, and it was full speed ahead.

Borglum began by making drawings, and from those he built **scale models**. Creating these smaller sculptures helped him work out glitches before attempting the final project. But he couldn't carve the real thing by himself. He needed workers who would be willing to hang from cliffs in dangerous and uncomfortable conditions. During much of the carving of Mount Rushmore, times were hard in the United States. Many people were desperate for jobs. So it was not hard to find hundreds of men willing to climb all over Mount Rushmore, even in harsh conditions, to get the job done and earn a paycheck.

Carving a Mountain

Borglum and his team would have to carve these huge faces into the rock accurately, without the help of computers or sophisticated tools. This would be a challenge.

The first thing the workers did was take measurements of the mountain cliff. Then Borglum used his tiny scale models to build larger versions that were exactly 12 times smaller than the faces that would be carved into the mountain. One inch on Borglum's final scale model equaled one foot on the mountain. To help transfer the design onto the mountainside, Borglum invented a special machine that pointed out the spots on the rock to be carved. Workers then marked those places with red paint.

After the mountain had been marked, they started blasting rock away to make the rough shapes of the faces. **Dynamite**, sticks that blow up when lit, was used most of the time to remove the rock. Before each blast, everyone had to climb down 700 steps to get off the mountain, and after the blast, they had to march right back up.

Borglum and his workers finished the rough shape of the George Washington sculpture in 1927.

Workers roughly carve out Lincoln's head. Crews worked in teams of 30 men. There were carvers, drillers, and machine operators on each team.

Workers spent a lot of time improving the monument after blasting. They worked hard to chip away rock that didn't get blasted off. They also polished the men's rock faces.

It's All in the Details

When the blasting was done, workers chiseled and drilled away more rock to place the men's features in the correct place and add fine details to the sculptures. Then they polished and smoothed the surfaces. The crew had to remove rock by hand from every inch of the four men's heads. It proved to be a huge and tiring task. Washington's face alone measured 60 feet from top to bottom. The crew worked in extreme heat and bitter cold. They had to dangle from thin cables hundreds of feet in the air, sometimes in windy weather, using heavy, powerful tools. Some workers couldn't stand the frightening height and brutal conditions, but many stuck it out to the end. Not a single worker died during this dangerous job.

Borglum didn't live to see his masterpiece completed, but his son, Lincoln Borglum, kept the work going. In 1941, after $1 million in expenses and 14 years of hard work, Robinson's dream for South Dakota became a reality. Today, more than two million people each year visit Mount Rushmore, making it the largest tourist attraction in South Dakota.

> Borglum (right) oversees a team of sculptors polishing the monument with sanding machines.

Check In Why did Borglum reject the first sites Robinson showed him in South Dakota? Why did they choose Mount Rushmore for their sculpture?

THE FACES
ON THE MOUNTAIN

by David Holford

It was hard to decide how to carve gigantic faces into the side of Mount Rushmore. But perhaps the biggest decision looming over Robinson and his team was which four historic faces to carve. Early in the process, Native American leaders and heroes from the American West were considered. But when Gutzon Borglum was hired as the sculptor of the project, he had already made up his mind. He would carve the images of four great presidents into the stone.

A recent photo shows the view of Mount Rushmore from the base of the monument.

George Washington

GUIDING OUR COUNTRY

George Washington is known as the father of our country. Washington began his career by fighting in a war against the French. Later, he used his military experience to lead the colonial army in the Revolutionary War. His leadership helped win America's independence from Britain. In 1789, he became the first president of the United States. As president, he chose the site of our nation's capital and restored peace with Britain after the war. To honor Washington's role in founding the nation, Borglum gave him a place at the front of the monument so his image would stand out from the others.

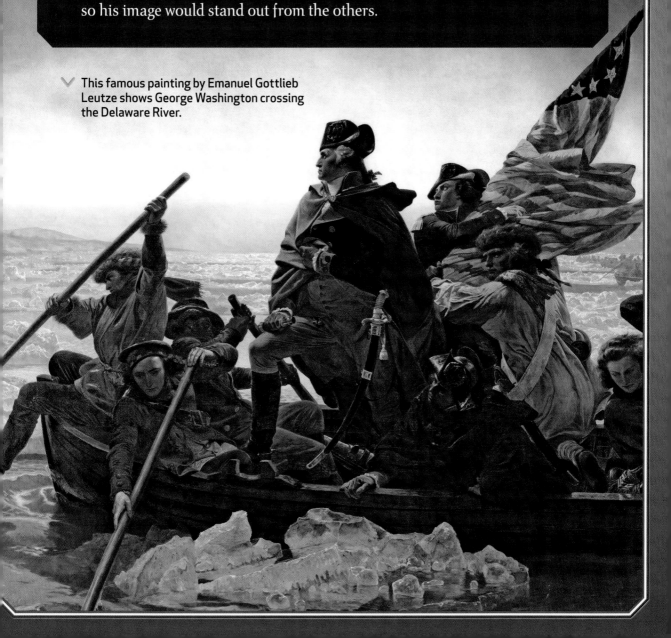

This famous painting by Emanuel Gottlieb Leutze shows George Washington crossing the Delaware River.

> Thomas Jefferson stands with a quill in his hand. Benjamin Franklin (far left) and John Adams sit as they review a draft of the Declaration of Independence.

Thomas Jefferson

EXPANDING OUR NATION

Next came Thomas Jefferson, who also played an important part in the nation's birth. In 1776, he wrote the Declaration of Independence, which declared to the British king that the American colonies would fight for their freedom. For Borglum, however, Jefferson earned his place on Mount Rushmore as the symbol of our nation's **expansion**, or growth.

As the third president, Jefferson bought the huge Louisiana Territory from France in 1803. The Louisiana Purchase doubled the size of the United States. The land that now makes up South Dakota, as well as all or part of 14 other present-day states, was part of the purchase. So, if it weren't for Jefferson, there wouldn't even be a South Dakota or a Mount Rushmore National Memorial.

Abraham Lincoln

Abraham Lincoln was chosen as a symbol of a united nation. In 1861, a great disagreement over states' rights, slavery, and other issues raged between the North and the South. Many people in the South had slaves. Many Northerners wanted an end to slavery. The disagreement caused Southern states to form their own separate country. They feared that President Lincoln would end slavery. Soon, a Civil War began between the North and the South. Determined to **preserve** the nation, Lincoln successfully worked to end the war and reunite the country.

Borglum originally planned to carve a short history of the United States on a huge tablet next to the faces on the monument. The tablet would be shaped like the land the United States gained through the Louisiana Purchase. But Borglum needed the space that had been reserved for the tablet to carve Lincoln's image instead.

Lincoln stands with two of his men after a battle in Maryland.

Theodore Roosevelt

Finally, Borglum placed Theodore Roosevelt on the mountain as a symbol of the United States' development as a world leader. Roosevelt championed the construction of a U.S.-controlled canal across the country of Panama in the early 1900s. The Panama Canal allowed ships to move quickly between the Atlantic and Pacific Oceans. It also made it easier for the United States to trade with countries around the world.

In the United States, Roosevelt worked hard to protect and preserve the nation's most beautiful sites. He set aside land for national parks, national forests, and the nation's first national monuments. Today, Mount Rushmore is part of the national park system that Roosevelt created.

Teddy Roosevelt loved nature. Here he rides on horseback through Yellowstone National Park.

One More Face?

DR. MARTIN
LUTHER KING, JR.

SUSAN B.
ANTHONY

ROSA
PARKS

AMELIA
EARHART

NEIL
ARMSTRONG

As Borglum worked on his monument, some people called for a fifth sculpture. They wanted to honor Susan B. Anthony for her fight for women's **suffrage**, or the right to vote. Congress even passed a law to include her on the monument. However, there was not enough money left to pay for this additional work.

Over the years, people have suggested that other important Americans be added to this popular landmark. Some want to include people who helped make sure that all Americans had equal rights, such as Dr. Martin Luther King, Jr. or Rosa Parks. Others want to honor American pioneers. Should we add Amelia Earhart, the first female pilot to fly across the Atlantic Ocean by herself? Or astronaut Neil Armstrong, the first person on the moon? If you could choose, who would you add to Mount Rushmore?

Check In Choose one of the figures on Mount Rushmore and explain how and why he was selected for the monument.

BLASTING THROUGH

by Jennifer A. Smith

Creating Mount Rushmore involved blasting away 450,000 tons of rock.

BOOM!

Rocks flew through the air! But the skilled workers on Mount Rushmore had everything under control. They were blasting rock to create art.

Most sculptors use chisels and other small tools to carve rock, but Mount Rushmore was mainly sculpted using dynamite and **jackhammers**. Workers on Mount Rushmore used dynamite to blast away the rock. Then they drilled a series of holes to make it easier to break down the rock. Finally, they would smooth out the rock until the features on each face were just right. But without dynamite, the faces would have been extremely difficult to carve.

Swedish chemist Alfred Nobel invented dynamite in 1867. He had worked with different **explosives** for several years, and he knew how dangerous they could be. A few years earlier, Nobel's brother had been killed in an explosion. Nobel mixed certain substances together to create a safer explosive he called dynamite. Dynamite, it turned out, was also easier to use than other explosives.

The timing of Nobel's invention was perfect. During the mid-1800s, the United States was growing bigger and bigger. Railroads, tunnels, and **canals**, or waterways, were being built around the expanding country for moving people and goods. For each project, workers needed to blast away great amounts of rock. Dynamite worked better than anything else to quickly carve out such large, heavy areas of rock. Who would have thought something as destructive as dynamite would be necessary to create an important piece of art like Mount Rushmore?

∧ This worker is carrying a lot of explosive power. Dynamite was safer to handle than the explosives people had been using.

The Panama Canal is a 40-mile route between the Atlantic and Pacific Oceans. Workers faced many dangers while building the canal.

60 million pounds of dynamite were used to build the Panama Canal.

More than 30 ships pass through the Panama Canal each day.

CONNECTING OCEANS

Dynamite wasn't important only for carving Mount Rushmore. It also helped American builders create many other great new projects.

At the time of dynamite's invention, ship captains were looking for a shortcut. Sailing from New York City, New York, all the way around South America to San Francisco, California, was taking too long. The ship captains wanted to find a way to cut across Central America.

In 1881, a French company made the first attempt at building what would later be called the Panama Canal. By connecting the Atlantic Ocean to the Pacific Ocean through Central America, the canal would save ships weeks of travel between the East and West. However, the company building the canal faced many problems along the way. Their equipment didn't work well on the rough land, and many workers fell ill from tropical diseases, such as malaria. The plan itself was flawed, and the attempt to build the canal failed.

In 1904, the United States took over the project. Despite the difficulty involved with building the canal, the United States managed to complete it by 1914, just ten years later. How did they do it? Dynamite. It took more than 60 million pounds of dynamite to carve out the land where the canal was constructed.

> This is a detonator box. It allows workers to explode dynamite from a distance. Pushing down the stick at the top of this box sends an electric charge to the dynamite. The charge sets off the explosives in the sticks of dynamite.

DIGGING ON THE DOUBLE

Not only can dynamite help build canals, it can help build tunnels, too. Today, thanks to dynamite, a train can travel right through a mountain in states such as Virginia and California. That's a lot quicker than going around or over the mountain.

Back in the 1850s, people wanted to find a way to transport goods across the Blue Ridge Mountains in the East to western states. To do this, they needed to build a railroad through the mountains that stood in the way. Because dynamite had not yet been invented, the original Blue Ridge Tunnel in Virginia was drilled and blasted by hand. Workers used hand drills, pickaxes, and a dangerous explosive called "black powder" to carve out the tunnel. Using this method, they could only dig a couple of feet each day. It took about six years to finish digging the tunnel. At the time of its completion, the Blue Ridge Tunnel was the longest railroad tunnel in the United States. It was more than 4,200 feet long.

Dynamite changed the pace at which workers could build tunnels. In 1874, work began on the Tehachapi Loop, part of a railroad line that would connect the San Francisco Bay area to Southern California. By using dynamite, some 3,000 workers were able to build 18 tunnels through the steep Tehachapi Mountains in only about two years.

> Dynamite blasts out rock for a railroad in Deadwood, South Dakota.

∨ Nobel named dynamite after the Greek word *dynamis*. This word means "power."

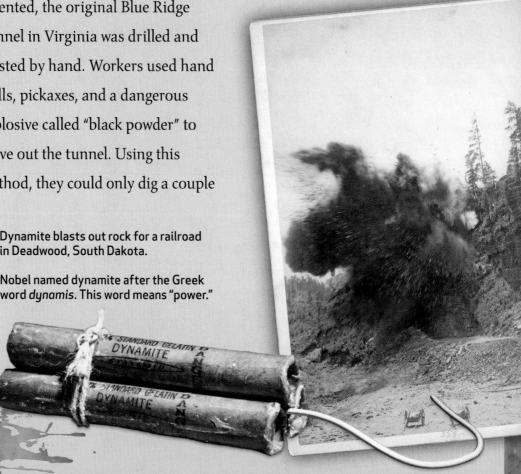

Every day about 40 trains pass through the 18 tunnels that make up the Tehachapi Loop.

Check In How was dynamite used to carve out the faces on the Mount Rushmore monument?

GENRE Opinion Piece

Read to find out two different views about the location and symbolic meaning of Mount Rushmore.

MOUNT RUSHMORE
OR
Six Grandfa

by *Debbie Nevins*

ers?

A man stands on a small hill near a Lakota settlement in South Dakota in 1891.

Mount Rushmore was named after a young lawyer named Charles Edward Rushmore. As far as many white settlers knew, the mountain had no other name. But to the Native American groups living in the area, that mountain *did* have a name. The Native Americans of the region were the Lakota, a group that belonged to a large nation known as the Sioux (SOO). The Lakota called the mountain "Six Grandfathers," and it was an important part of their history and heritage. Native Americans considered all of the Black Hills **sacred**, or important to their religion. They traveled to the mountains to perform spiritual ceremonies. The mountains were also part of their traditional homeland.

When Gutzon Borglum carved the faces of the U.S. presidents on Six Grandfathers, many Native Americans were upset. It was bad enough that, years before, U.S. settlers and soldiers had taken sacred lands away from the Native Americans and forced them to move onto areas of land called reservations. But now, they felt the U.S. government had spoiled the land they used to call home.

Most U.S. citizens see the monument on Mount Rushmore as a proud **symbol** of a great nation. Many Native Americans, however, see it as a symbol of destruction, one that shows disrespect toward their culture.

THIS LAND IS MY LAND

How does one group of people take land away from another? The Lakota people had lived in the Black Hills for hundreds of years before Europeans arrived there. As more Europeans intruded on their land, the Lakota attacked them to discourage people from settling there. In order to stop the attacks, the U.S. government signed a **treaty**, or agreement, in 1868. The treaty promised the Black Hills to the Lakota forever—but forever turned out to be a short time. Just four years later, when miners found gold in the hills, the United States went back on its promise and forced the Lakota from the Black Hills.

This painting shows the Battle of the Little Bighorn. This battle was fought in 1876. Lakota heroes Sitting Bull and Crazy Horse defeated U.S. troops led by George Armstrong Custer. It was one of many battles between the Lakota and U.S. troops.

The Lakota fought to keep their homeland. A series of bloody battles, sometimes called the Black Hills War, followed. Ultimately, the Native Americans were no match for the U.S. Army, and in 1877, the Lakota were forced to give up their land.

A century later, in 1980, the U.S. Supreme Court agreed the land had been taken from the Lakota illegally. The Court awarded the Lakota people $106 million, but it did not give them back the land. Today, that settlement money has grown to more than one billion dollars, but the Lakota have never collected it. They don't want the money, they say. They want what is rightfully theirs: the Black Hills. Over the years, the Lakota have staged several protests at Mount Rushmore, explaining to tourists that they will never take the money because "the Black Hills are not for sale!"

Native Americans protest to make it clear that they will not sell their land.

WHAT DO YOU THINK?

The battles over the Black Hills happened a long time ago, but the conflict over the use of the land is still going on today. Meanwhile, Native Americans and the U.S. government have tried to come up with ways to help make the situation better.

Let's Build Our Own Monument

In 1939, Chief Henry Standing Bear hired a sculptor to create a memorial honoring Lakota hero Crazy Horse. It would be a mountain monument even larger than Mount Rushmore. The Crazy Horse project began in 1948, but it has been slow going. The granite rock is difficult to carve and the organizers have refused to take government funds to help pay for it. Called "the largest mountain carving in progress," it remains far from complete.

Start the Healing

When Gerard Baker became the first Native American superintendent of the Mount Rushmore National Memorial in 2004, he asked **tribal elders** for advice. He wanted to find a way to bring Native American and U.S. cultures together in a balanced and respectful way. Thanks to his efforts, today the park includes Heritage Village, where Native Americans teach tourists about traditional Lakota ways of life.

"We're promoting all cultures of America," Baker says. "That's what this place is. This is Mount Rushmore! It's America! Everybody's something different here; we're all different. And just maybe that gets us talking again as human beings, as Americans."

The face of Crazy Horse stands 87 feet tall. When the monument is completed, Crazy Horse will be 563 feet tall. That's almost two times taller than the Statue of Liberty.

Gerard Baker stands in front of Mount Rushmore. He has worked at many national parks. He feels the parks are important. They demonstrate how people can share and enjoy the same land peacefully.

Check In   Why have many Native Americans been unhappy about Mount Rushmore?

RUSHMORE ROCKS!

by Jennifer A. Smith

Mount Rushmore is a powerful symbol of the founding and growth of the United States. Often, you see it in items from our **popular culture**. Popular, or "pop," culture includes movies, TV shows, and many other things that are popular in our country. Here are a few ways Mount Rushmore has popped up in pop culture.

⌄ Paperweights, mugs, and T-shirts—visitors often bring home one or more **souvenirs** (soo-vuh-NIHRZ), or reminders, of their visit to Mount Rushmore.

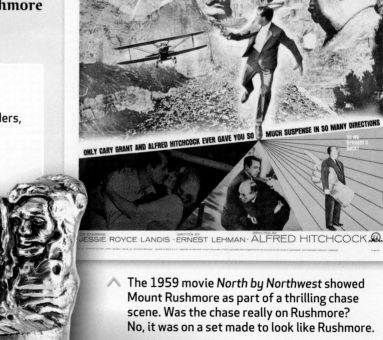

△ The 1959 movie *North by Northwest* showed Mount Rushmore as part of a thrilling chase scene. Was the chase really on Rushmore? No, it was on a set made to look like Rushmore.

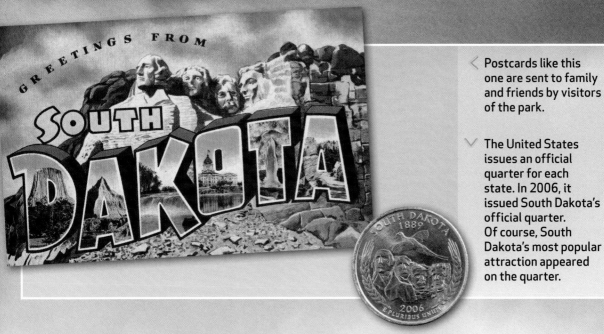

Postcards like this one are sent to family and friends by visitors of the park.

The United States issues an official quarter for each state. In 2006, it issued South Dakota's official quarter. Of course, South Dakota's most popular attraction appeared on the quarter.

Denmark's LEGOLAND PARK has models of the world's most famous landmarks. Mount Rushmore made the cut! It's the largest LEGO model in the park. This plastic version of the monument is made of about 1.5 million LEGO bricks and 40,000 DUPLO bricks.

One artist chose Mount Rushmore as the subject of a Los Angeles mural for the Fourth of July. What better way to celebrate the day the United States gained its independence from Britain than showing a monument that features two of our nation's founders?

Check In How has Mount Rushmore become an important part of American popular culture?

Discuss

1. What connections can you make among the five selections in this book? How are the selections linked?

2. Describe two important things you have learned about the process by which the Mount Rushmore monument was created.

3. What do you think about Borglum's decision to change the subject matter of the monument from heroes of the West to the presidents of the United States?

4. Consider the issues surrounding the Mount Rushmore National Memorial, which remains on traditional Lakota land. What is your opinion about the location of this memorial?

5. What do you still want to know about Mount Rushmore?